POP & MOVIE HITS

75 **Short Late Elementary Piano Solos**
with Optional Duet Accompaniments

Arranged by Tom Gerou

A to Z

All titles in this book are proven to be time-tested favorites from a variety of musical styles that can be enjoyed by both kids and adults. Care has been given to help make the music easy to play. The pieces are engraved in facing-page formats. All selections are arranged in traditional five-finger style, with the melody split between the hands—no hands-together playing—and without key signatures in the solo part. Dotted quarter notes, triplets and sixteenth notes have been avoided. When there are lyrics, leader lines are also omitted to maintain an uncluttered look. All melodic arrangements have optional duet accompaniments for the fullest sound and maximum playing fun!

Produced by
Alfred Music Publishing Co., Inc.
P.O. Box 10003
Van Nuys, CA 91410-0003
alfred.com

ISBN-10: 0-7390-9145-X
ISBN-13: 978-0-7390-9145-6

Cover Art
Miscellaneous multimedia icons: © Shutterstock / Alexander Lukin

 Alfred Cares. Contents printed on 100% recycled paper.

Contents

Anakin's Theme

from *Star Wars Episode I: The Phantom Menace*

Music by **JOHN WILLIAMS**

Arr. by Tom Gerou

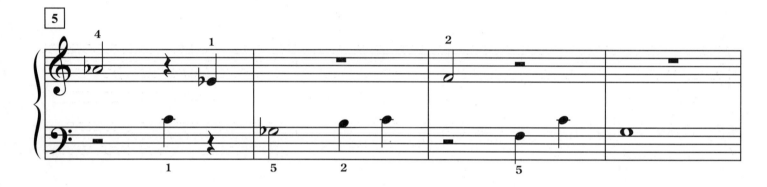

Optional Duet Accompaniment (Play solo part 1 octave higher than written.)

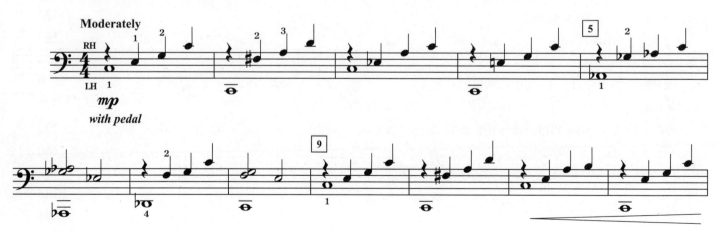

Annie's Song

Words and Music by John Denver

Arr. by Tom Gerou

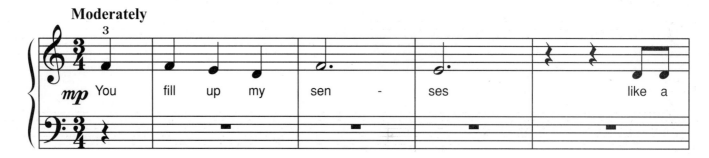

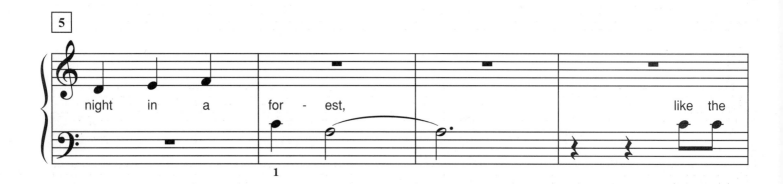

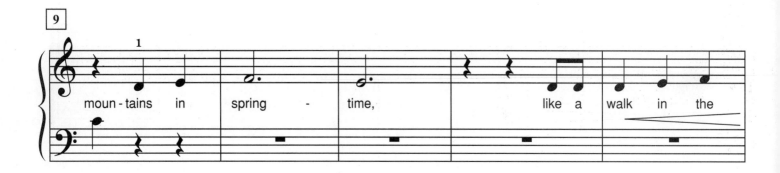

Optional Duet Accompaniment (Play solo part 1 octave higher than written.)

Beat It

Written and Composed by
Michael Jackson

Arr. by Tom Gerou

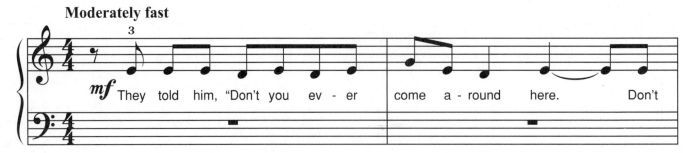

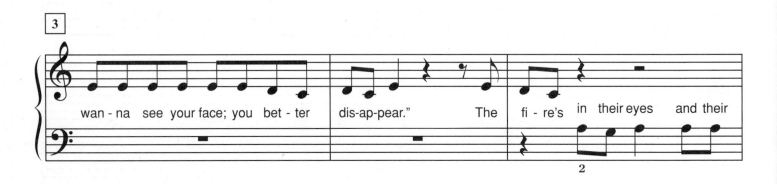

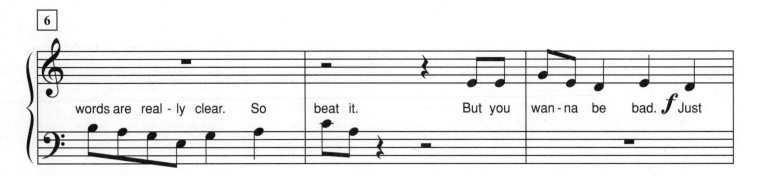

Optional Duet Accompaniment (Play solo part 1 octave higher than written.)

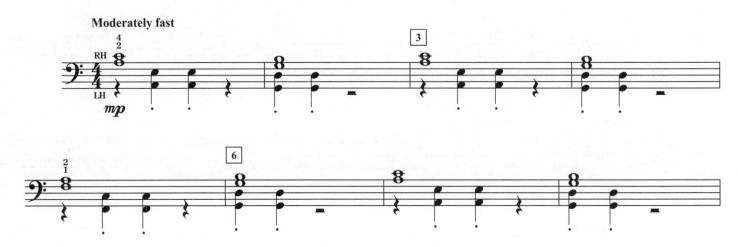

Bye Bye Love

Words and Music by
Boudleaux Bryant and Felice Bryant

Arr. by Tom Gerou

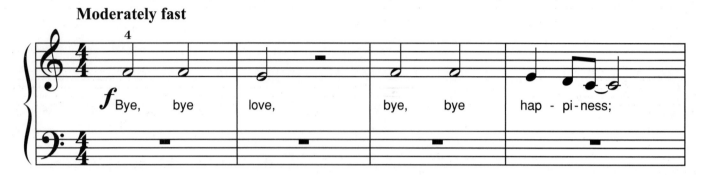

Bye, bye love, bye, bye hap - pi - ness;

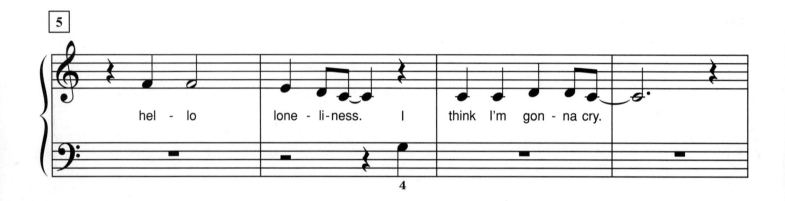

hel - lo lone - li - ness. I think I'm gon - na cry.

Optional Duet Accompaniment (Play solo part 1 octave higher than written.)

Cantina Band

from *Star Wars Episode IV: A New Hope*

Music by **JOHN WILLIAMS**

Arr. by Tom Gerou

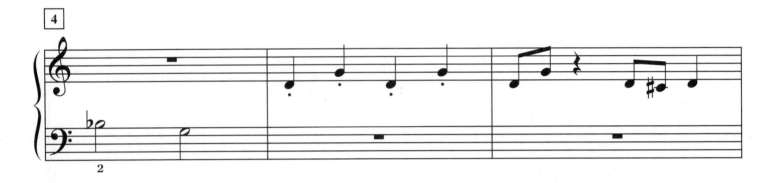

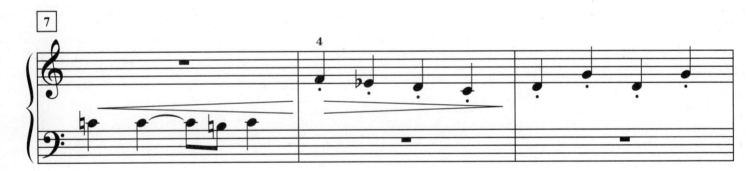

Optional Duet Accompaniment (Play solo part 1 octave higher than written.)

Cleopha (March and Two-Step)

Scott Joplin

Arr. by Tom Gerou

March tempo

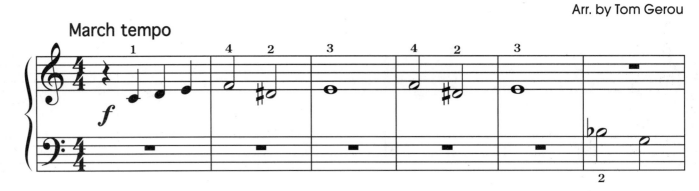

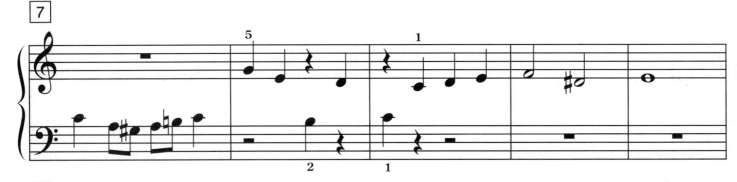

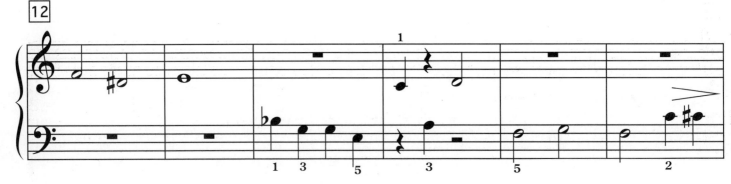

Optional Duet Accompaniment (Play solo part 1 octave higher than written.)

March tempo

Colors of the Wind

from Walt Disney's *Pocahontas*

Lyrics by Stephen Schwartz
Music by Alan Menken

Arr. by Tom Gerou

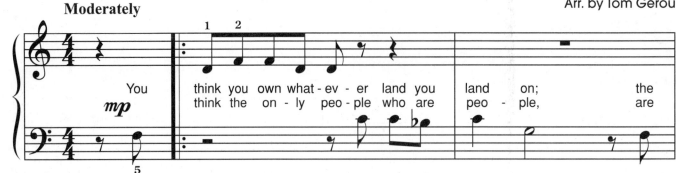

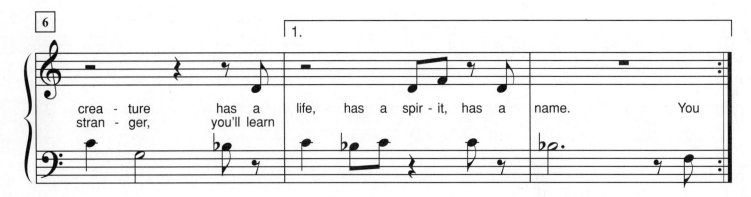

Optional Duet Accompaniment (Play solo part 1 octave higher than written.)

Ding-Dong! The Witch Is Dead

from *The Wizard of Oz*

Lyrics by E. Y. Harburg
Music by Harold Arlen

Arr. by Tom Gerou

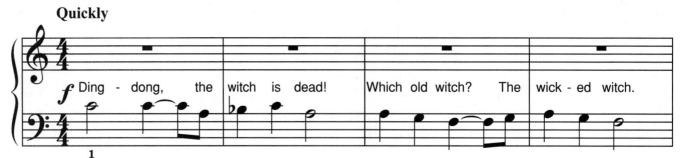

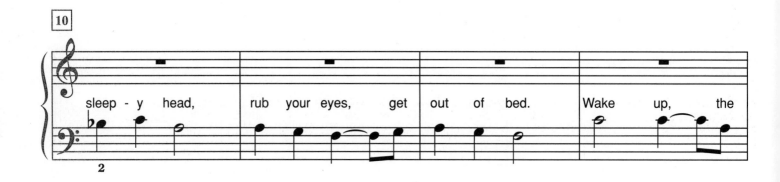

Optional Duet Accompaniment (Play solo part 1 octave higher than written.)

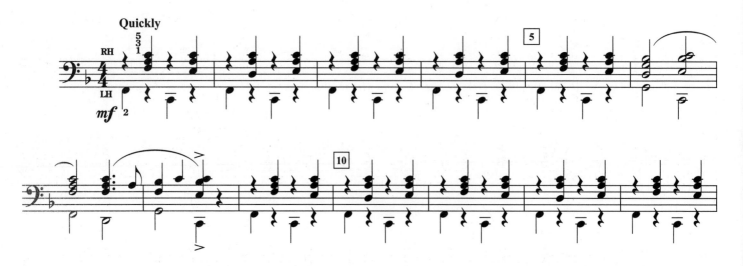

Don't Stop Believin'

Words and Music by Jonathan Cain,
Neal Schon and Steve Perry

Arr. by Tom Gerou

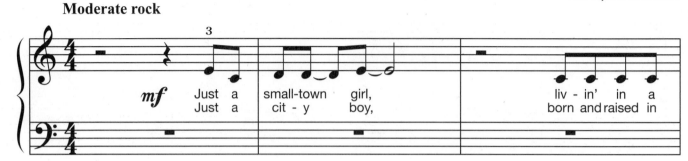

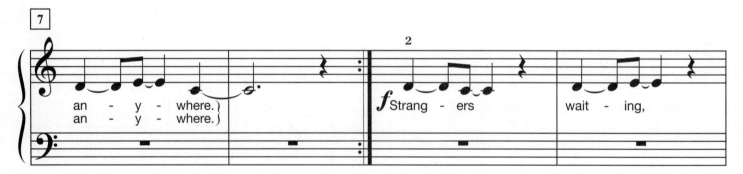

Optional Duet Accompaniment (Play solo part 1 octave higher than written.)

Duel of the Fates

from *Star Wars Episode I: The Phantom Menace*

Music by **JOHN WILLIAMS**

Arr. by Tom Gerou

Fast, with great force

Optional Duet Accompaniment (Play solo part 1 octave higher than written.)

Fast, with great force

The Entertainer

Scott Joplin

Arr. by Tom Gerou

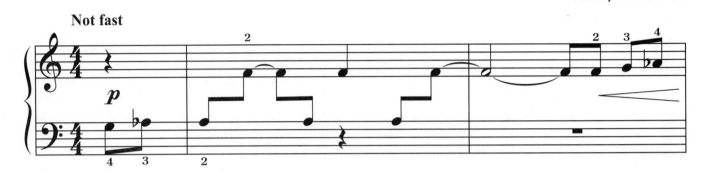

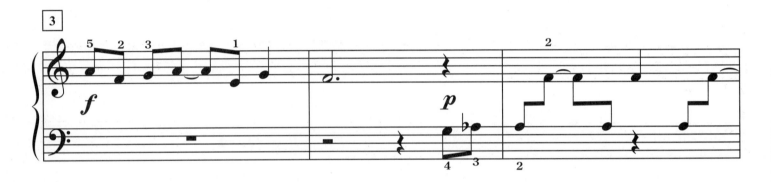

Optional Duet Accompaniment (Play solo part 1 octave higher than written.)

(Meet)
The Flintstones

Words and Music by
Joseph Barbera, William Hanna and Hoyt Curtin

Arr. by Tom Gerou

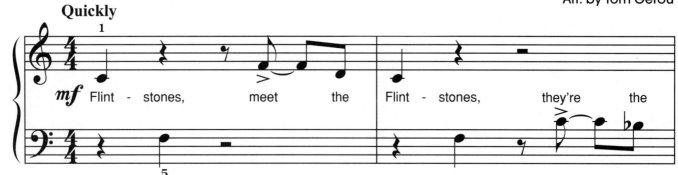

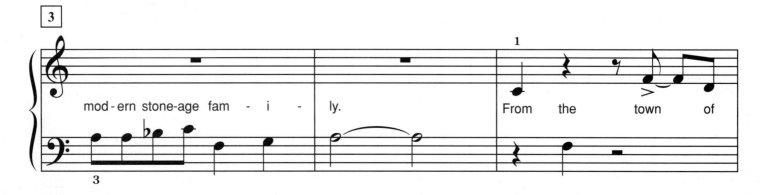

Optional Duet Accompaniment (Play solo part 1 octave higher than written.)

Funeral March of a Marionette

By Charles Gounod

Arr. by Tom Gerou

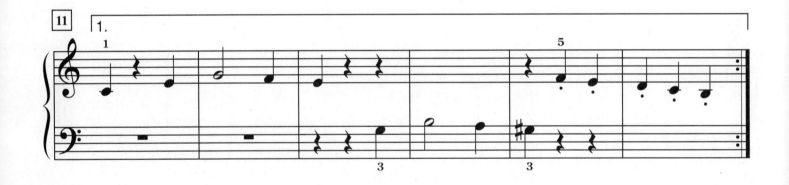

Optional Duet Accompaniment (Play solo part 1 octave higher than written.)

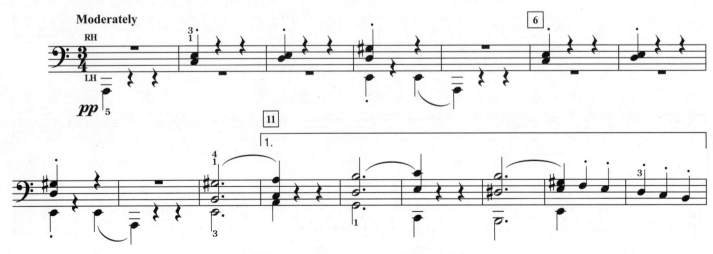

Georgy Girl

Words by Jim Dale
Music by Tom Springfield

Arr. by Tom Gerou

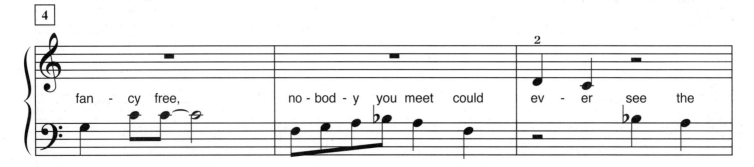

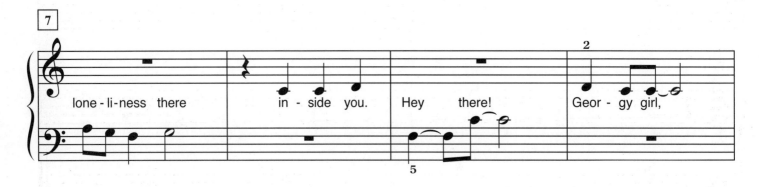

Optional Duet Accompaniment (Play solo part 1 octave higher than written.)

Ghostbusters

Words and Music by Ray Parker Jr.

Arr. by Tom Gerou

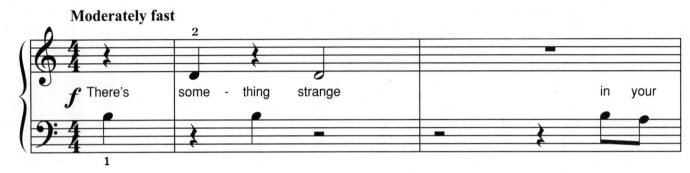

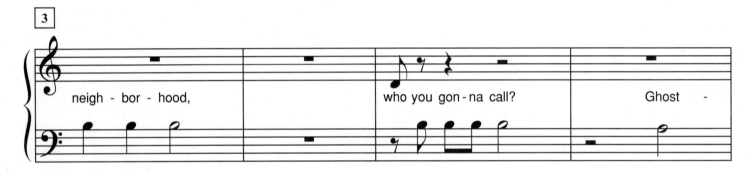

Optional Duet Accompaniment (Play solo part 1 octave higher than written.)

Grim Grinning Ghosts

from The Haunted Mansion at Disneyland Park and Magic Kingdom Park

Words by Xavier Atencio
Music by Buddy Baker

Arr. by Tom Gerou

Optional Duet Accompaniment (Play solo part 1 octave higher than written.)

Harry's Wondrous World
from *Harry Potter and the Sorcerer's Stone*

Music by **JOHN WILLIAMS**

Arr. by Tom Gerou

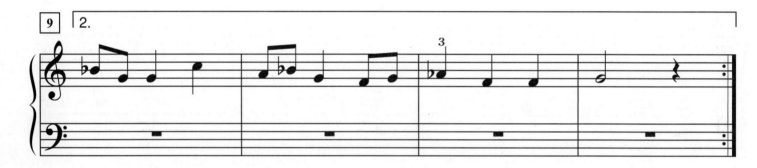

Optional Duet Accompaniment (Play solo part 1 octave higher than written.)

Heal the World

Written and Composed by Michael Jackson

Arr. by Tom Gerou

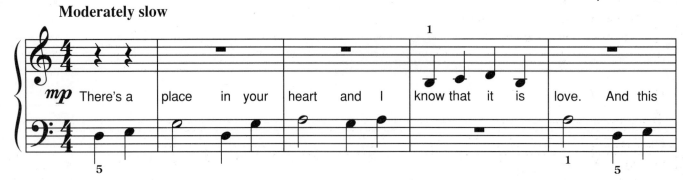

Optional Duet Accompaniment (Play solo part 1 octave higher than written.)

Hogwarts' Hymn

from *Harry Potter and the Goblet of Fire*

Music by Patrick Doyle

Arr. by Tom Gerou

Noble and expressive

Optional Duet Accompaniment (Play solo part 1 octave higher than written.)

Noble and expressive

with pedal

I Got Rhythm

Music and Lyrics by
George Gershwin and Ira Gershwin

Arr. by Tom Gerou

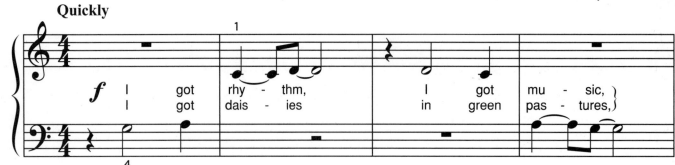

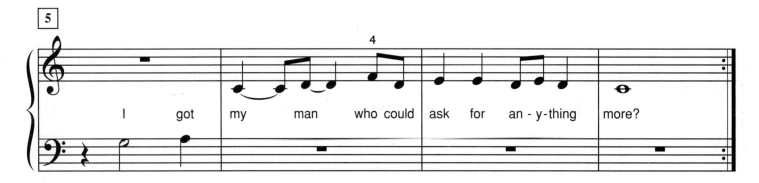

Optional Duet Accompaniment (Play solo part 1 octave higher than written.)

I Got You Babe

Words and Music by Sunny Bono

Arr. by Tom Gerou

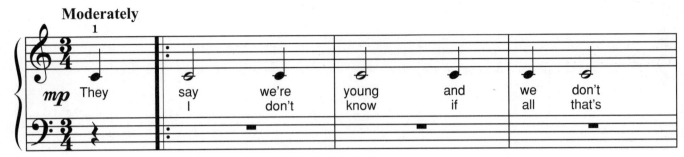

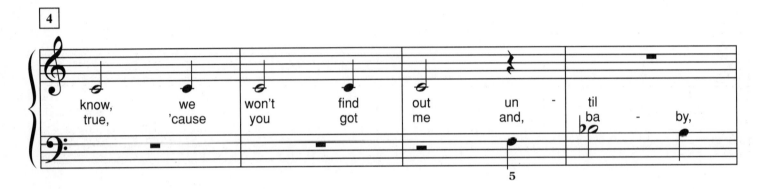

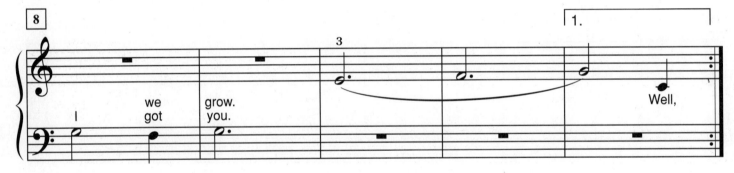

Optional Duet Accompaniment (Play solo part 1 octave higher than written.)

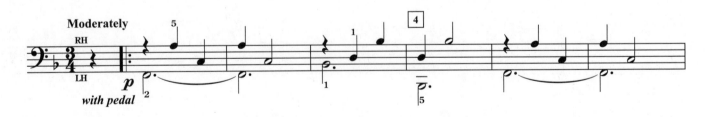

I Taut I Taw a Puddy Tat

from *Looney Tunes / Merrie Melodies*

Words and Music by
Alan Livingston, Billy May and Warren Foster

Arr. by Tom Gerou

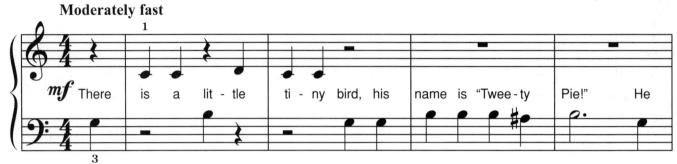

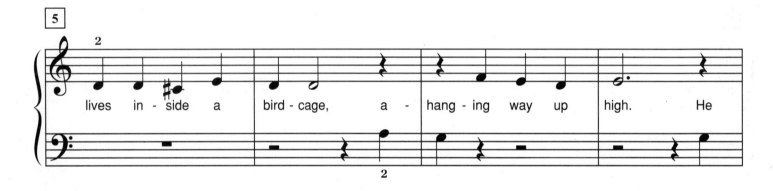

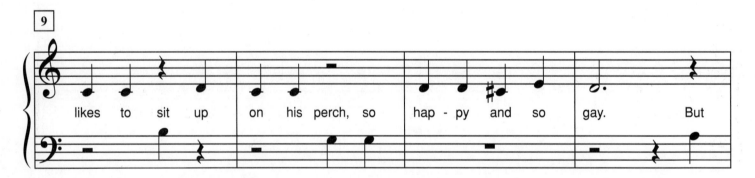

Optional Duet Accompaniment (Play solo part 1 octave higher than written.)

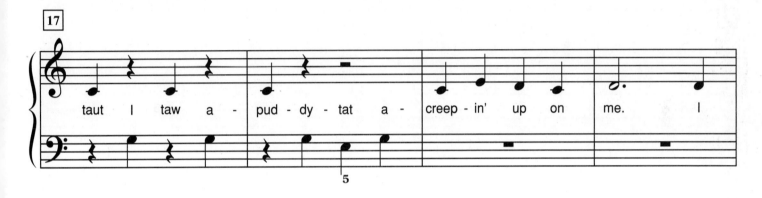

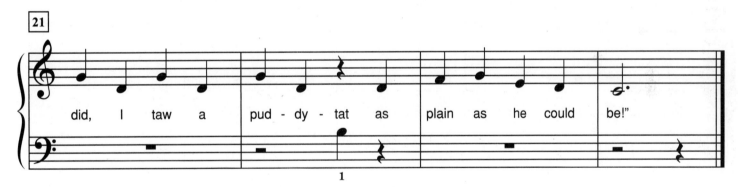

I Won't Grow Up

Lyrics by Carolyn Leigh
Music by Mark Charlap

Arr. by Tom Gerou

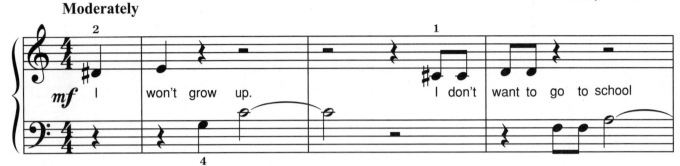

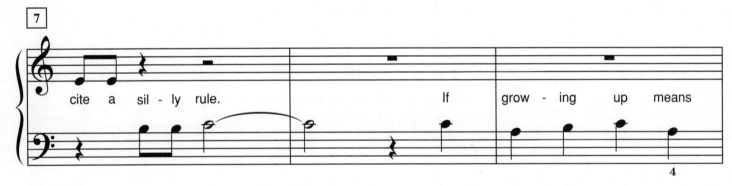

Optional Duet Accompaniment (Play solo part 1 octave higher than written.)

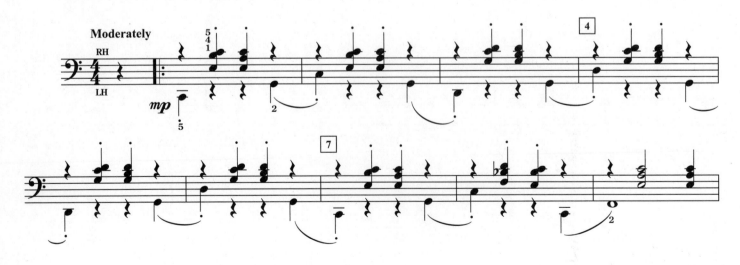

it would be be - neath my dig - ni - ty to climb a tree, I'll

nev - er grow up, nev - er grow up, nev - er grow up, no

sir, not I, not me, I won't, no sir!

If I Didn't Have You

from *Monsters, Inc.*

Words and Music by Randy Newman

Arr. by Tom Gerou

Moderate swing tempo

If I were a rich man with a mil-lion or two.

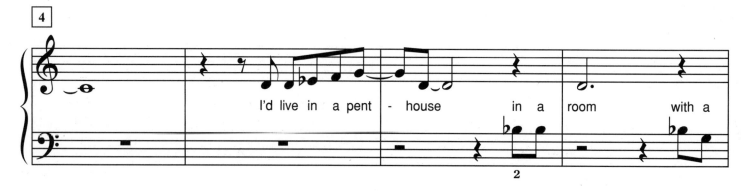

I'd live in a pent-house in a room with a

view. And if I were hand-some,

Optional Duet Accompaniment (Play solo part 1 octave higher than written.)

Moderate swing tempo

If I Only Had a Brain

from *The Wizard of Oz*

Lyrics by E. Y. Harburg
Music by Harold Arlen
Arr. by Tom Gerou

Optional Duet Accompaniment (Play solo part 1 octave higher than written.)

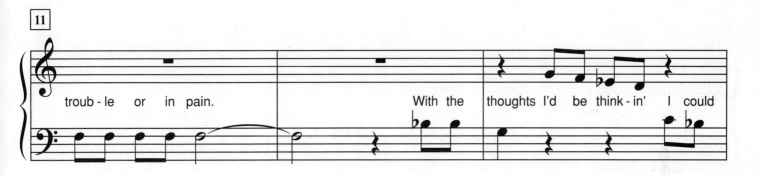

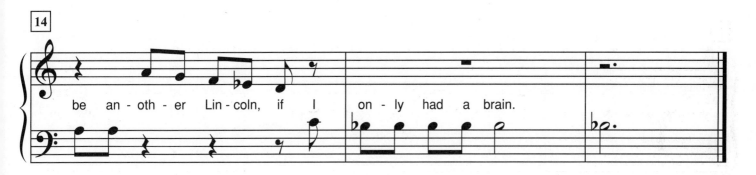

The Imperial March (Darth Vader's Theme)

from *Star Wars Episode V: The Empire Strikes Back*

Music by **JOHN WILLIAMS**

Arr. by Tom Gerou

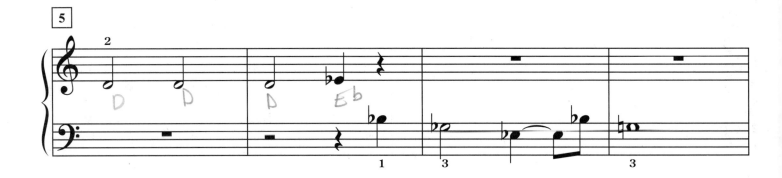

Optional Duet Accompaniment (Play solo part 1 octave higher than written.)

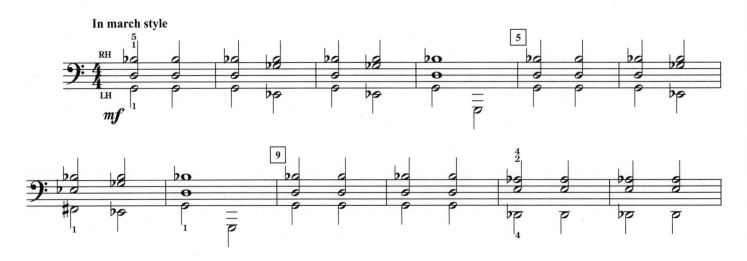

Inspector Gadget (Main Title)

Words and Music by
Haim Saban and Shuki Levy

Arr. by Tom Gerou

Moderate swing tempo

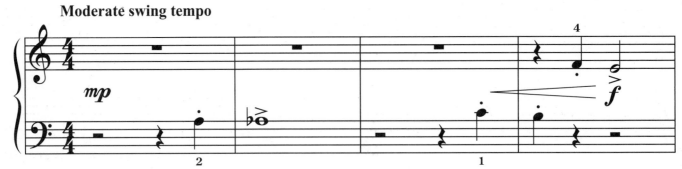

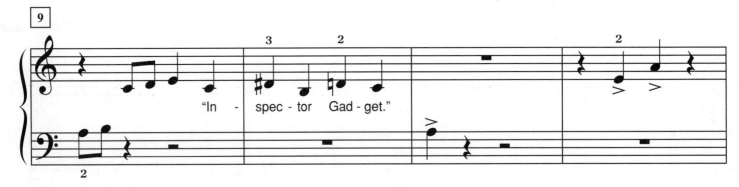

"In - spec - tor Gad - get."

Optional Duet Accompaniment (Play solo part 1 octave higher than written.)

Moderate swing tempo

It's My Party

Words and Music by Herb Wiener,
John Gluck and Wally Gold

Arr. by Tom Gerou

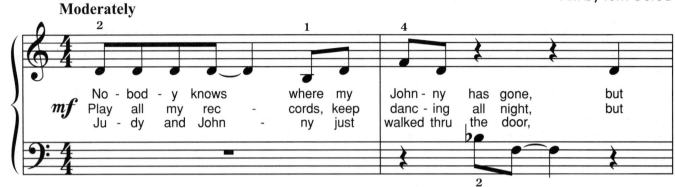

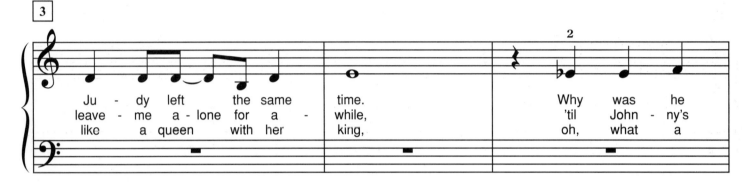

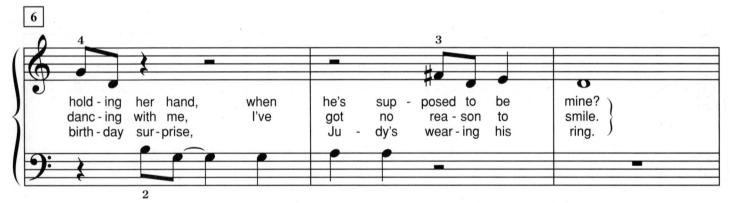

Optional Duet Accompaniment (Play solo part 1 octave higher than written.)

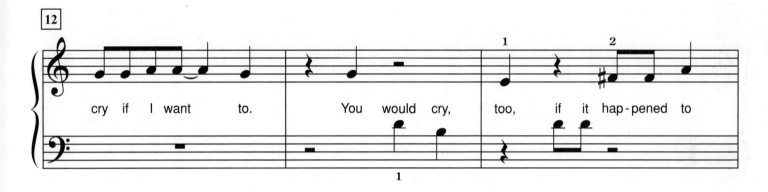

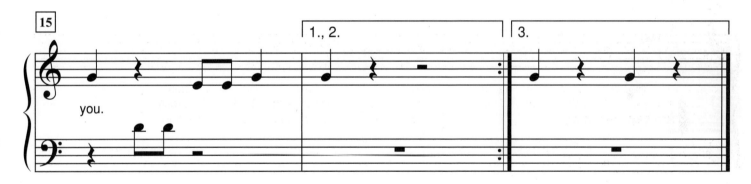

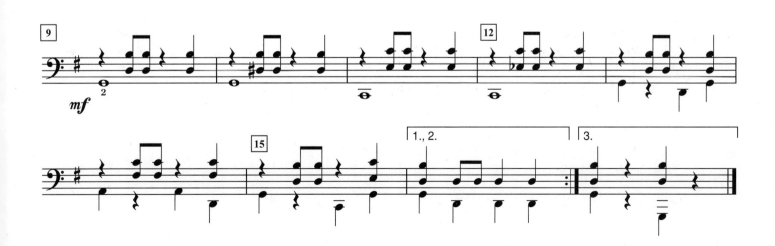

James Bond Theme

By Monty Norman

Arr. by Tom Gerou

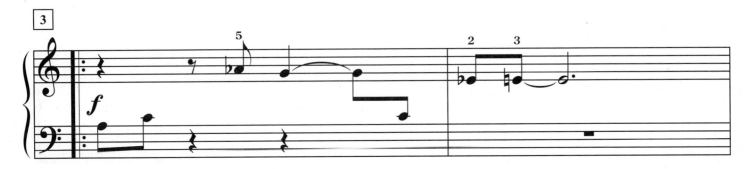

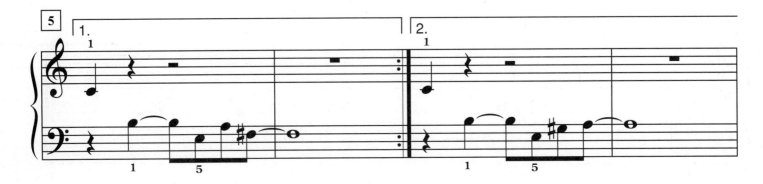

Optional Duet Accompaniment (Play solo part 1 octave higher than written.)

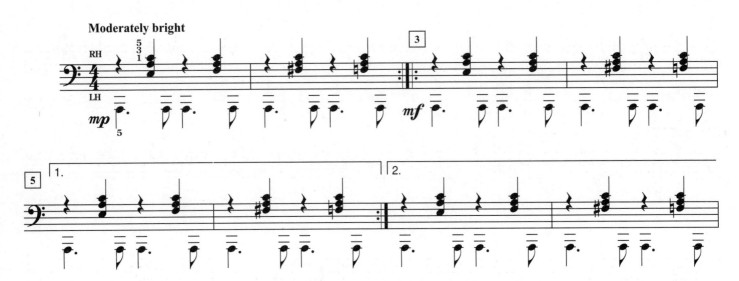

Jeepers Creepers

Words by Johnny Mercer
Music by Harry Warren

Arr. by Tom Gerou

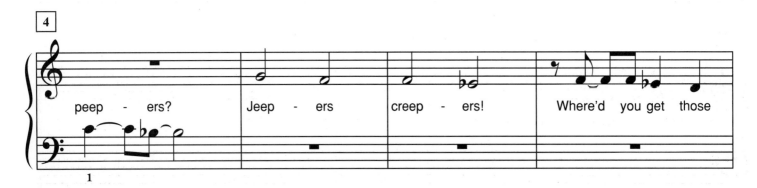

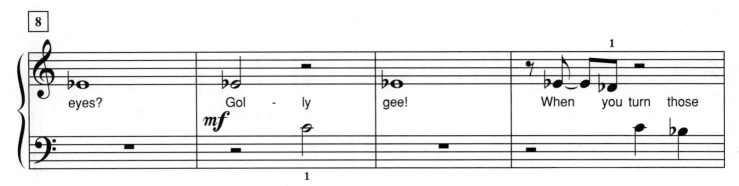

Optional Duet Accompaniment (Play solo part 1 octave higher than written.)

Killing Me Softly With His Song

Words and Music by
Charles Fox and Norman Gimbel

Arr. by Tom Gerou

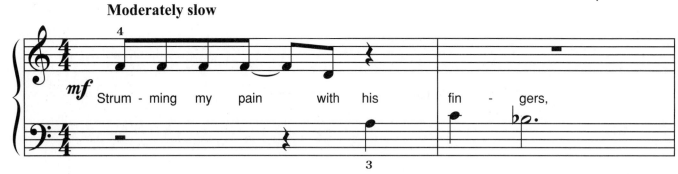

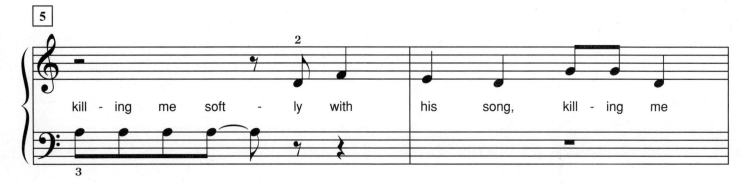

Optional Duet Accompaniment (Play solo part 1 octave higher than written.)

Let's Call the Whole Thing Off

Music and Lyrics by
George Gershwin and Ira Gershwin

Arr. by Tom Gerou

Quick swing tempo

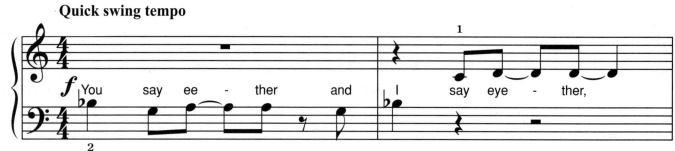

Optional Duet Accompaniment (Play solo part 1 octave higher than written.)

Quick swing tempo

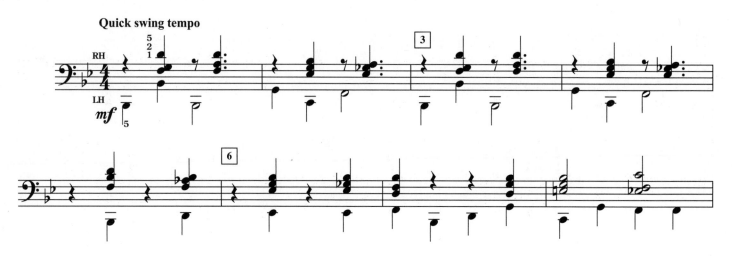

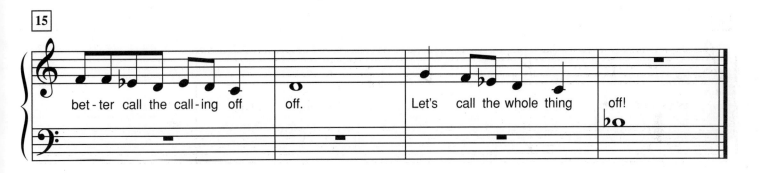

Lily's Lullaby

from *Harry Potter and the Deathly Hallows, Part 2*

By Alexandre Desplat

Arr. by Tom Gerou

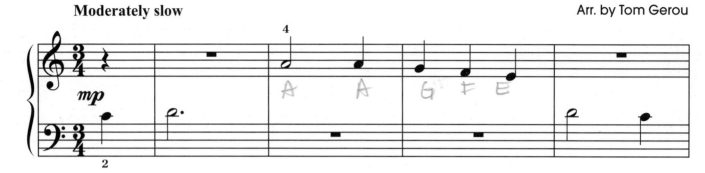

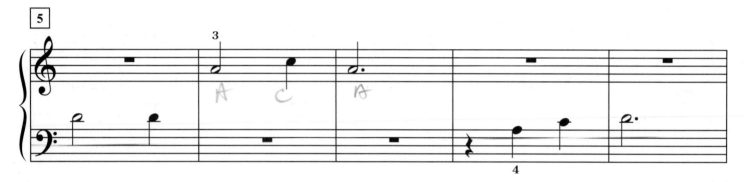

Optional Duet Accompaniment (Play solo part 1 octave higher than written.)

The Lion Sleeps Tonight

New Lyric and Revised Music by
George David Weiss, Hugo Peretti and Luigi Creatore

Arr. by Tom Gerou

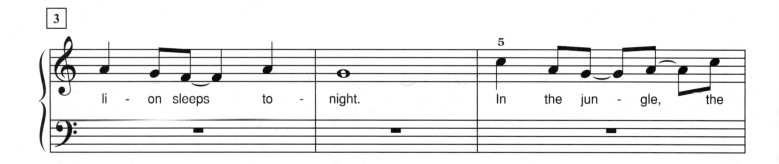

Optional Duet Accompaniment (Play solo part 1 octave higher than written.)

Luke and Leia

from *Star Wars Episode VI: Return of the Jedi*

Music by **JOHN WILLIAMS**

Arr. by Tom Gerou

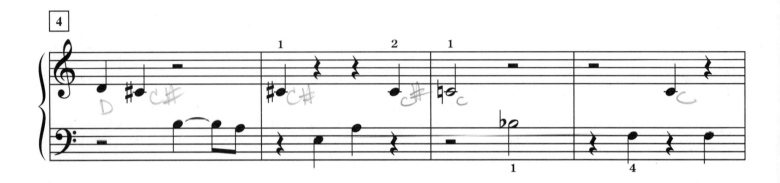

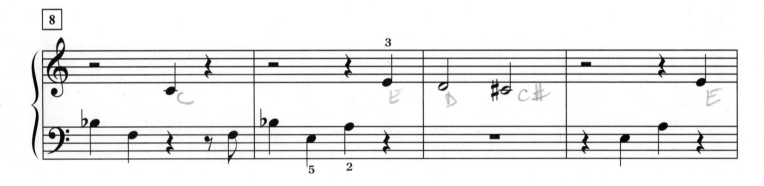

Optional Duet Accompaniment (Play solo part 1 octave higher than written.)

Mamma Mia
from *Mamma Mia!*

Words and Music by Benny Andersson,
Stig Anderson and Bjorn Ulvaeus

Arr. by Tom Gerou

Mam - ma Mi - a,   here I go a - gain.

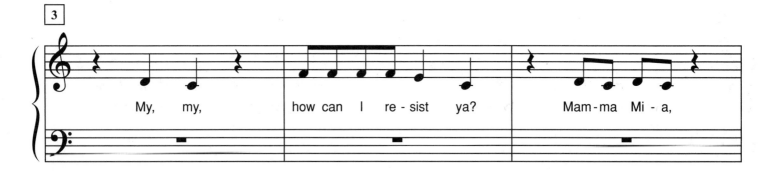

My,   my,   how can I re - sist ya?   Mam - ma Mi - a,

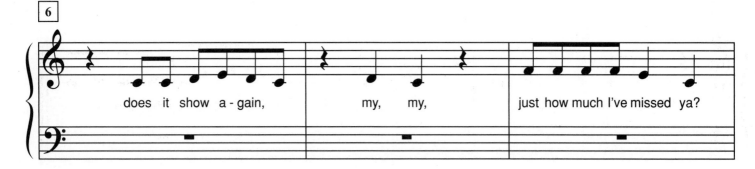

does it show a - gain,   my,   my,   just how much I've missed ya?

Optional Duet Accompaniment (Play solo part 1 octave higher than written.)

Maple Leaf Rag

Scott Joplin

Arr. by Tom Gerou

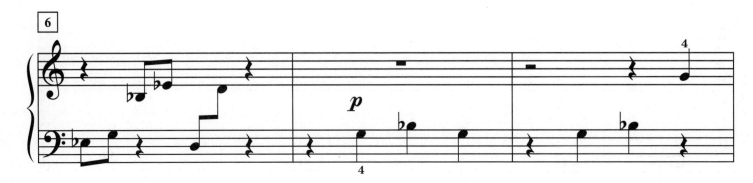

Optional Duet Accompaniment (Play solo part 1 octave higher than written.)

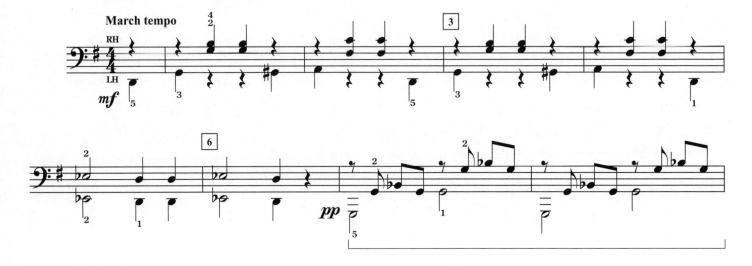

May the Force Be with You

from *Star Wars Episode V: The Empire Strikes Back*

Music by **JOHN WILLIAMS**

Arr. by Tom Gerou

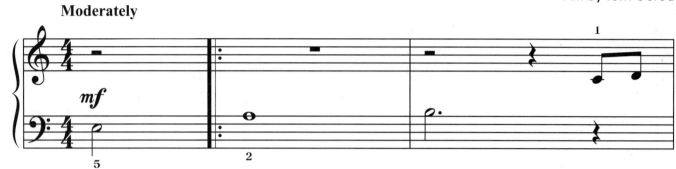

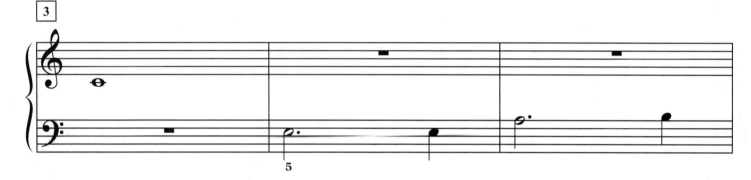

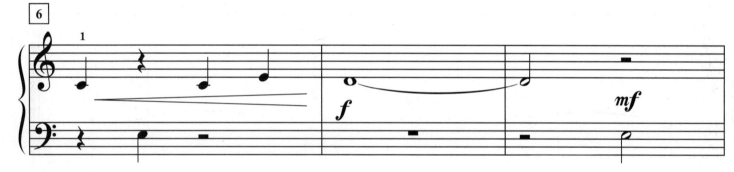

Optional Duet Accompaniment (Play solo part 1 octave higher than written.)

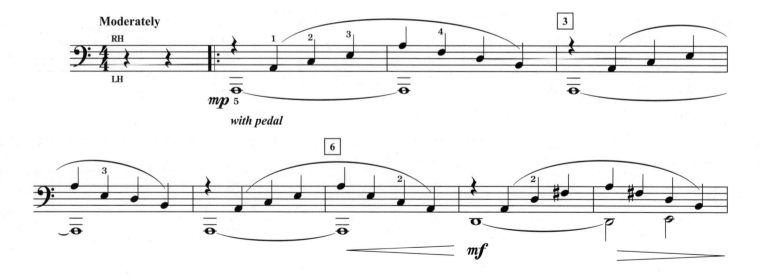

Merrily We Roll Along

from *Looney Tunes / Merrie Melodies*

Words and Music by Eddie Cantor,
Charlie Tobias, and Murray Mencher

Arr. by Tom Gerou

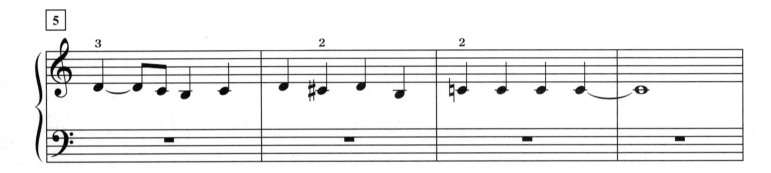

Optional Duet Accompaniment (Play solo part 1 octave higher than written.)

The Merry-Go-Round Broke Down

from Looney Tunes / Merrie Melodies

Words and Music by
Cliff Friend and Dave Franklin

Arr. by Tom Gerou

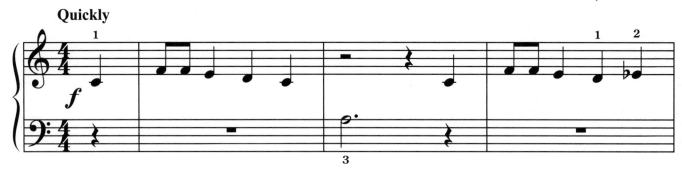

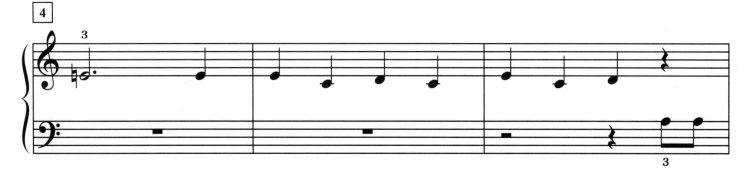

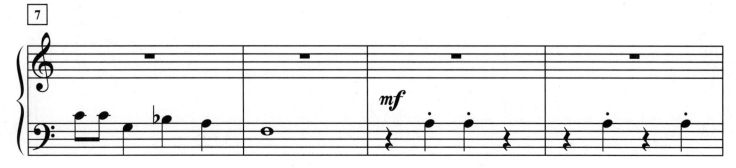

Optional Duet Accompaniment (Play solo part 1 octave higher than written.)

Mickey Mouse March

from Walt Disney's *The Mickey Mouse Club*

Words and Music by Jimmie Dodd

Arr. by Tom Gerou

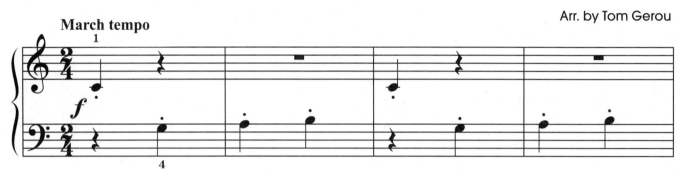

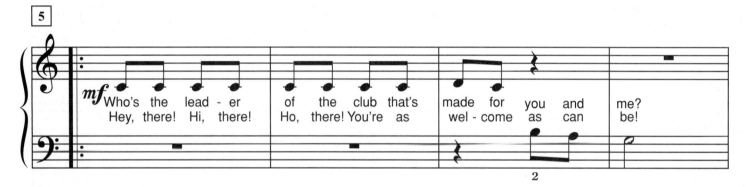

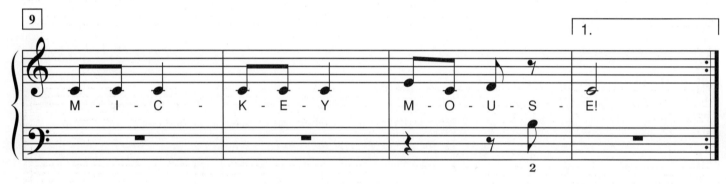

Optional Duet Accompaniment (Play solo part 1 octave higher than written.)

Monster Mash

Words and Music by
Bobby Pickett and Leonard Capizzi

Arr. by Tom Gerou

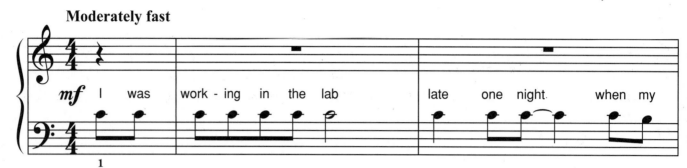

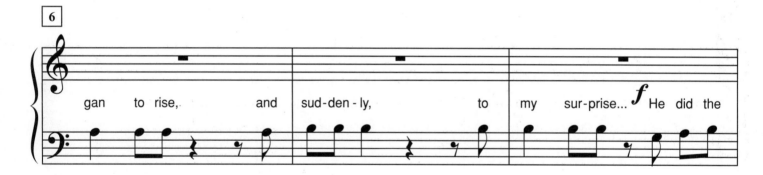

Optional Duet Accompaniment (Play solo part 1 octave higher than written.)

Need You Now

Words and Music by Dave Haywood,
Charles Kelley, Hillary Scott and Josh Kear

Arr. by Tom Gerou

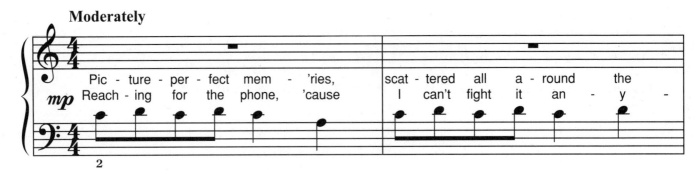

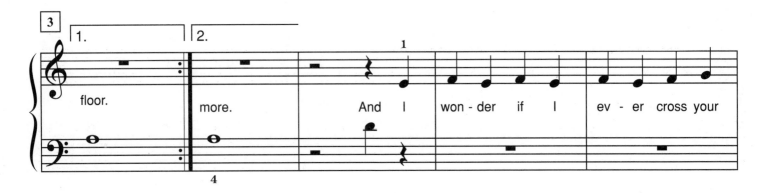

Optional Duet Accompaniment (Play solo part 1 octave higher than written.)

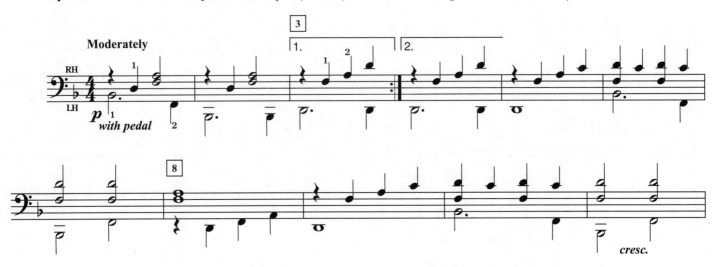

quar-ter af-ter one,   I'm   all   a-lone and I   need you now.   I

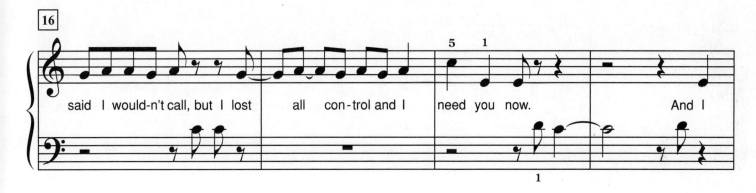

said I would-n't call, but I lost   all   con-trol and I   need you now.   And I

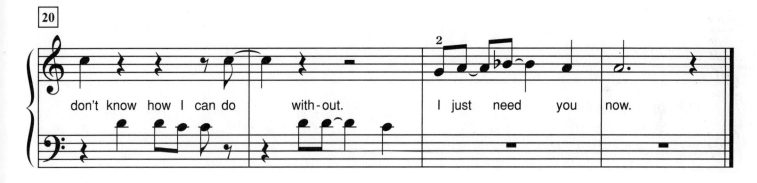

don't know how I can do   with-out.   I just   need   you   now.

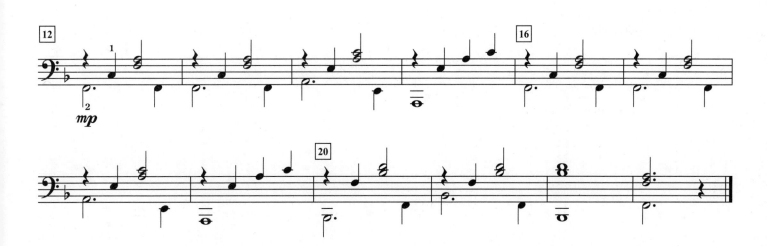

mp

Theme from **New York, New York**

Words by Fred Ebb
Music by John Kander

Arr. by Tom Gerou

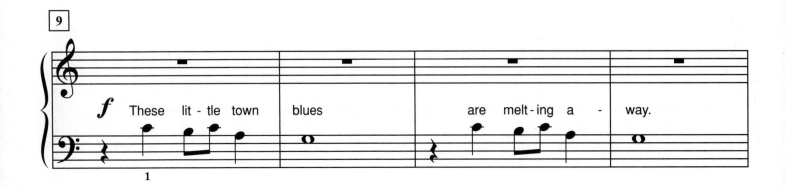

Optional Duet Accompaniment (Play solo part 1 octave higher than written.)

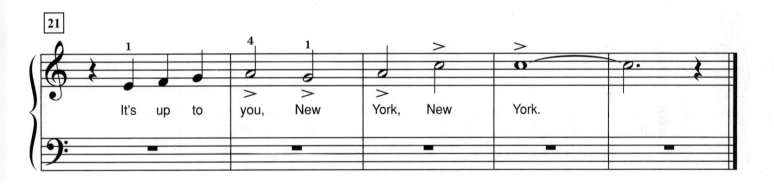

Nice Work If You Can Get It

Music and Lyrics by
George Gershwin and Ira Gershwin

Arr. by Tom Gerou

Moderate swing tempo

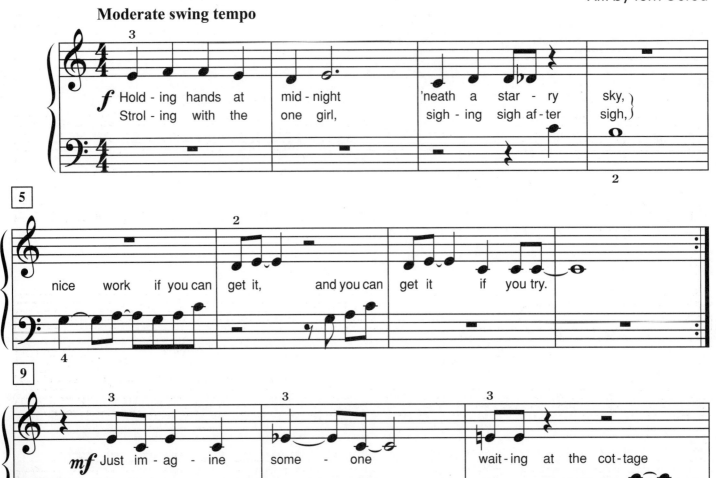

Optional Duet Accompaniment (Play solo part 1 octave higher than written.)

Moderate swing tempo

Optimistic Voices (You're Out of the Woods)

from *The Wizard of Oz*

Lyrics by E. Y. Harburg
Music by Harold Arlen
Arr. by Tom Gerou

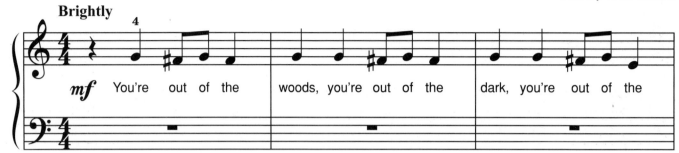

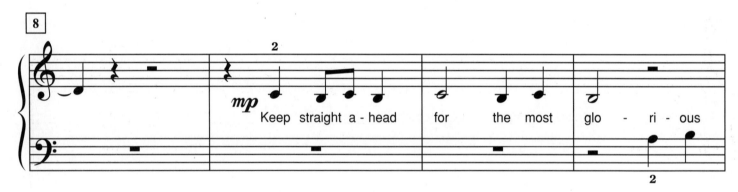

Optional Duet Accompaniment (Play solo part 1 octave higher than written.)

Over the Rainbow

from *The Wizard of Oz*

Lyrics by E. Y. Harburg
Music by Harold Arlen

Arr. by Tom Gerou

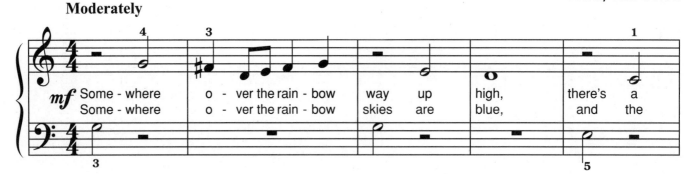

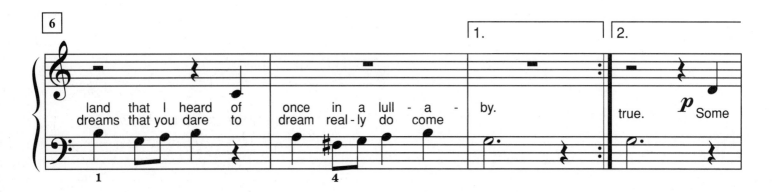

Optional Duet Accompaniment (Play solo part 1 octave higher than written.)

The Pink Panther

from *The Pink Panther*

By Henry Mancini

Arr. by Tom Gerou

Optional Duet Accompaniment (Play solo part 1 octave higher than written.)

Puff (The Magic Dragon)

Words and Music by
Peter Yarrow and Leonard Lipton

Arr. by Tom Gerou

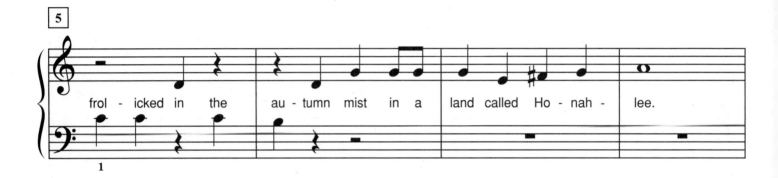

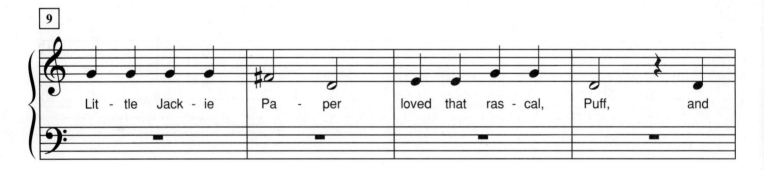

Optional Duet Accompaniment (Play solo part 1 octave higher than written.)

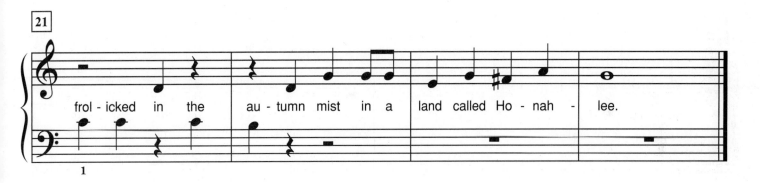

The Purple People Eater

Words and Music by Sheb Wooley

Arr. by Tom Gerou

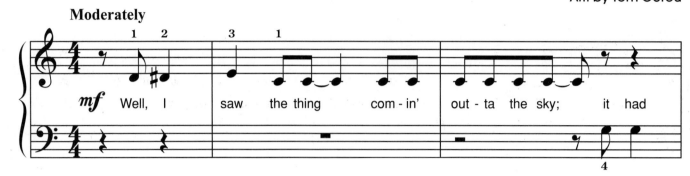

Well, I saw the thing com-in' out-ta the sky; it had

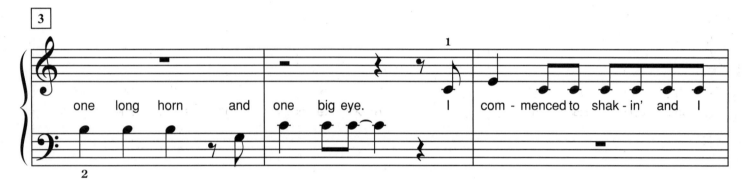

one long horn and one big eye. I com-menced to shak-in' and I

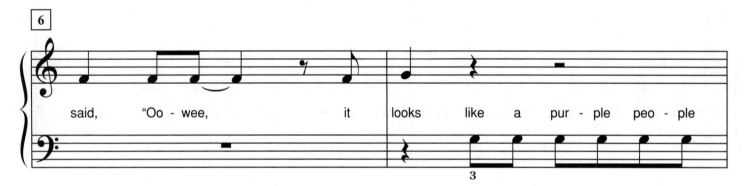

said, "Oo - wee, it looks like a pur-ple peo-ple

Optional Duet Accompaniment (Play solo part 1 octave higher than written.)

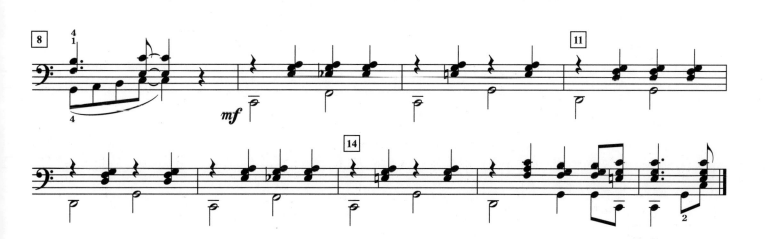

The Quidditch World Cup (The Irish)

from *Harry Potter and the Goblet of Fire*

Music by Patrick Doyle

Arr. by Tom Gerou

Optional Duet Accompaniment (Play solo part 1 octave higher than written.)

Raiders March

from *Indiana Jones and the Kingdom of the Crystal Skull*

Music by **JOHN WILLIAMS**

Arr. by Tom Gerou

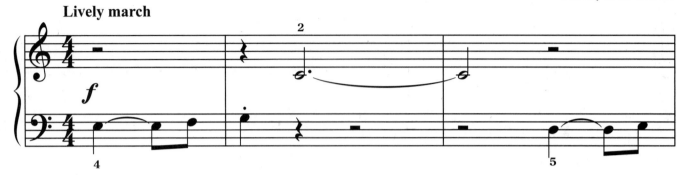

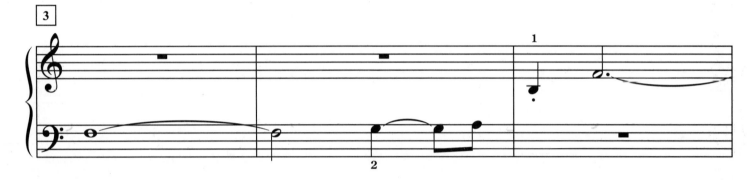

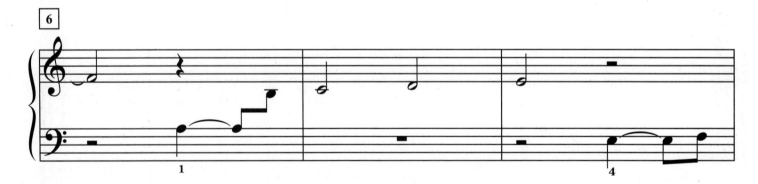

Optional Duet Accompaniment (Play solo part 1 octave higher than written.)

Raindrops Keep Fallin' on My Head

Words by Hal David
Music by Burt Bacharach

Arr. by Tom Gerou

Optional Duet Accompaniment (Play solo part 1 octave higher than written.)

thing I know, the blues they send to meet me won't de-

feat me. It won't be long till hap - pi - ness steps

up to greet me. Be - cause I'm free,

noth - in's wor - ry - in' me.

rit. *mp*

rit. *p*

(We're Gonna)
Rock Around the Clock

Words and Music by
Max C. Freedman and Jimmy De Knight

Arr. by Tom Gerou

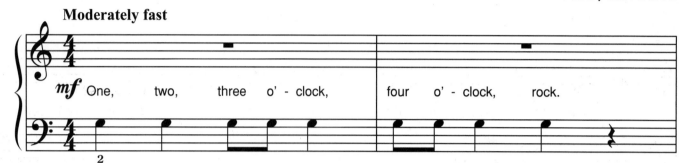

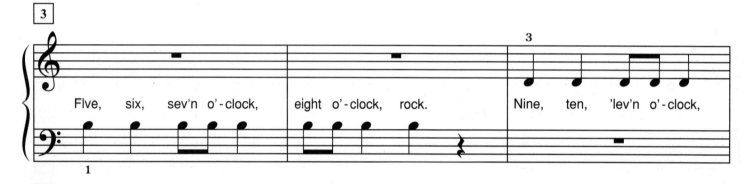

Optional Duet Accompaniment (Play solo part 1 octave higher than written.)

Scooby Doo, Where Are You?

Words and Music by
David Mook and Ben Raleigh

Arr. by Tom Gerou

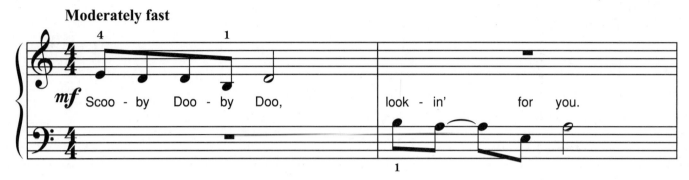

Optional Duet Accompaniment (Play solo part 1 octave higher than written.)

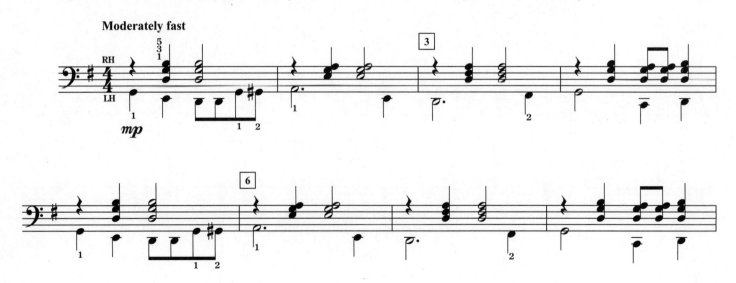

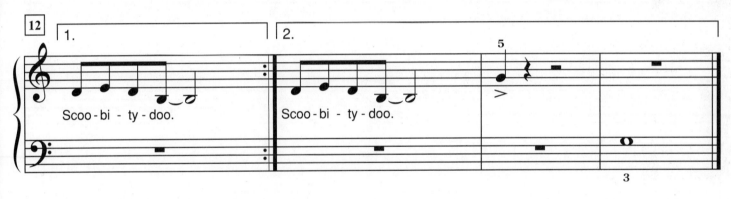

Solace (A Mexican Serenade)

Scott Joplin

Arr. by Tom Gerou

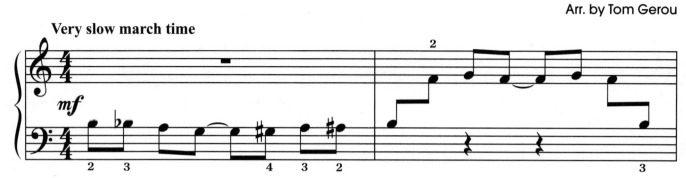

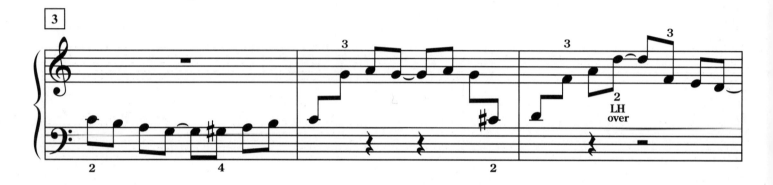

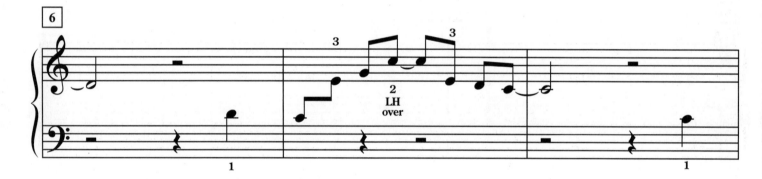

Optional Duet Accompaniment (Play solo part 1 octave higher than written.)

The Sorcerer's Apprentice

By Paul Dukas

Arr. by Tom Gerou

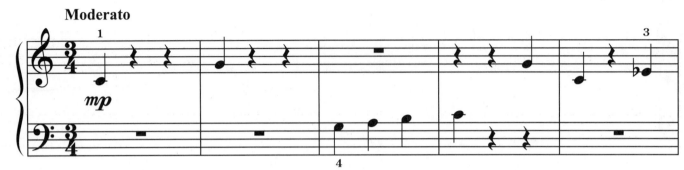

Optional Duet Accompaniment (Play solo part 1 octave higher than written.)

The Sound of Silence

Words and Music by Paul Simon

Arr. by Tom Gerou

Hel - lo, dark - ness, my old friend,

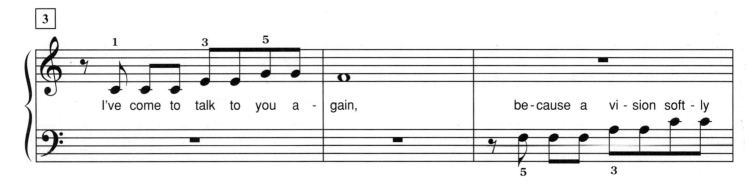

I've come to talk to you a - gain, be - cause a vi - sion soft - ly

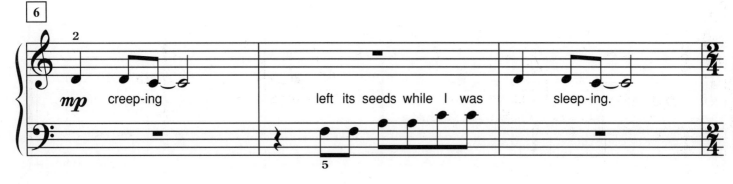

creep-ing left its seeds while I was sleep-ing.

Optional Duet Accompaniment (Play solo part 1 octave higher than written.)

Splish Splash

Words and Music by
Bobby Darin and Jean Murray

Arr. by Tom Gerou

Moderately, with a beat

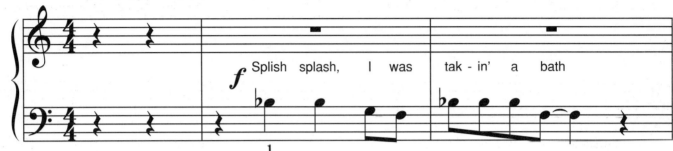

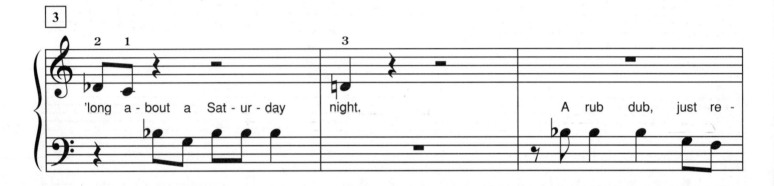

Optional Duet Accompaniment (Play solo part 1 octave higher than written.)

Moderately, with a beat

Star Wars (Main Theme)

from *Star Wars Episode IV: A New Hope*

Music by **JOHN WILLIAMS**

Arr. by Tom Gerou

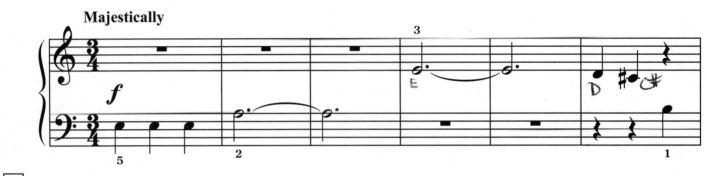

Optional Duet Accompaniment (Play solo part 1 octave higher than written.)

Strike Up the Band!

Music and Lyrics by
George Gershwin and Ira Gershwin

Arr. by Tom Gerou

Moderate swing tempo

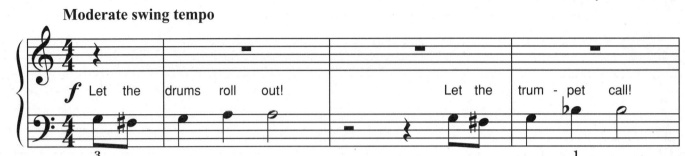

Optional Duet Accompaniment (Play solo part 1 octave higher than written.)

Moderate swing tempo

Summertime

from *Porgy and Bess*

Music and Lyrics by
George Gershwin, Ira Gershwin and
Du Bose and Dorothy Heyward

Arr. by Tom Gerou

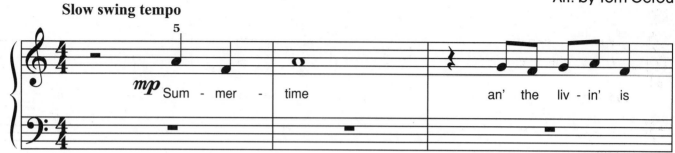

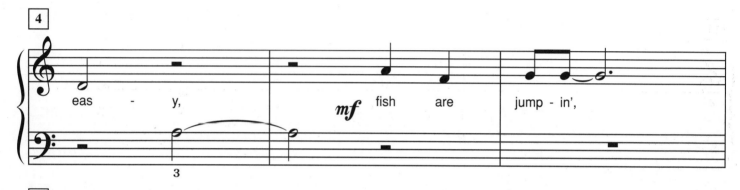

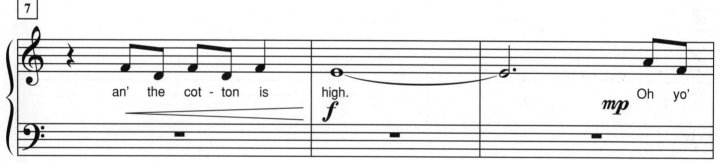

Optional Duet Accompaniment (Play solo part 1 octave higher than written.)

Sunshine on My Shoulders

Words by John Denver
Music by John Denver, Mike Taylor and Dick Kniss

Arr. by Tom Gerou

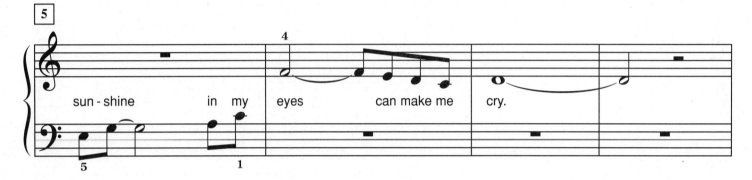

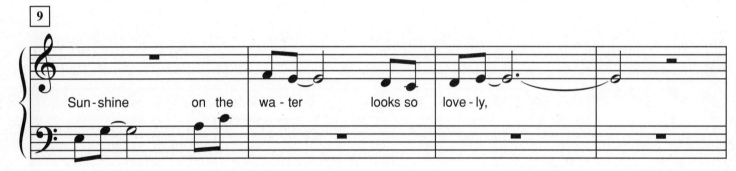

Optional Duet Accompaniment (Play solo part 1 octave higher than written.)

Theme from
Superman

Music by **JOHN WILLIAMS**

Arr. by Tom Gerou

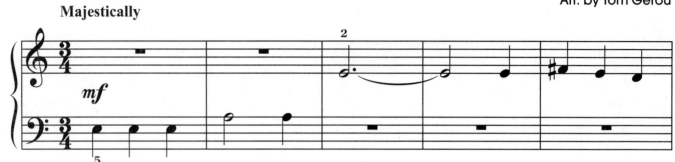

Optional Duet Accompaniment (Play solo part 1 octave higher than written.)

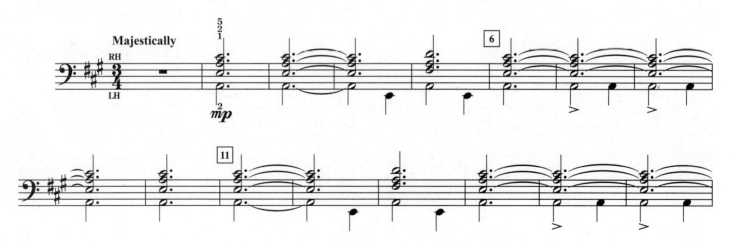

A Teenager in Love

Words by Doc Pomus
Music by Mort Shuman

Arr. by Tom Gerou

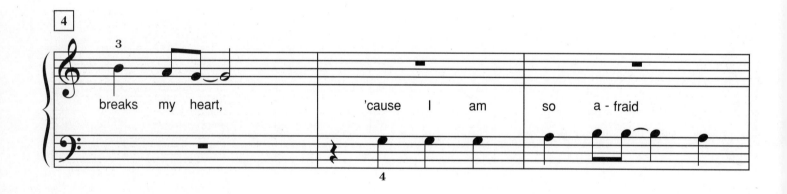

Optional Duet Accompaniment (Play solo part 1 octave higher than written.)

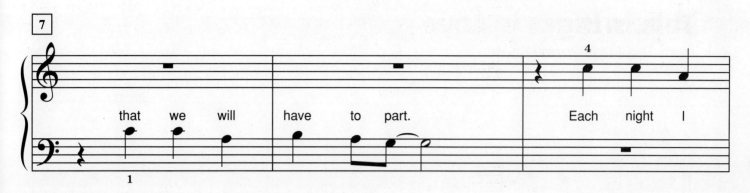

that we will have to part. Each night I

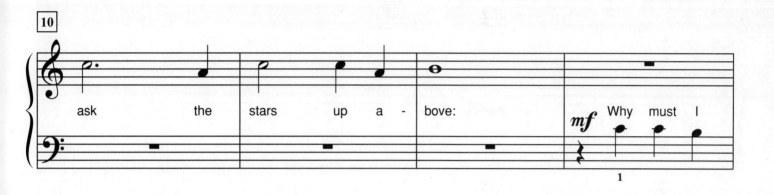

ask the stars up a - bove: *mf* Why must I

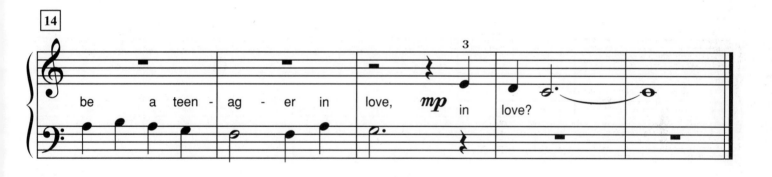

be a teen - ag - er in love, *mp* in love?

This Is It!

from *The Bugs Bunny Show*

Words and Music by
Mack David and Jerry Livingston

Arr. by Tom Gerou

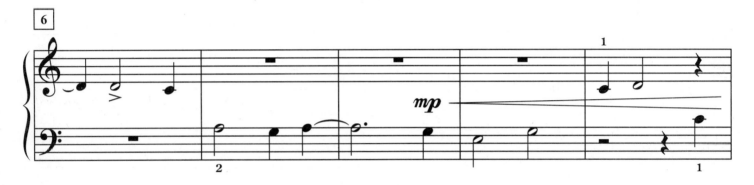

Optional Duet Accompaniment (Play solo part 1 octave higher than written.)

Voldemort

from *Harry Potter and the Sorcerer's Stone*

Music by **JOHN WILLIAMS**

Arr. by Tom Gerou

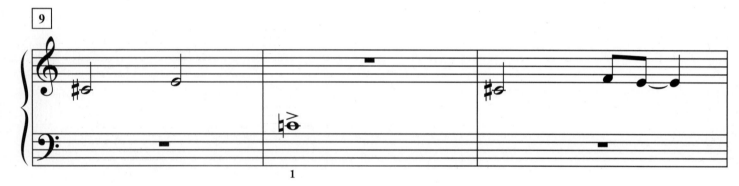

Optional Duet Accompaniment (Play solo part 1 octave higher than written.)

We're Off to See the Wizard

from *The Wizard of Oz*

Lyrics by E. Y. Harburg
Music by Harold Arlen

Arr. by Tom Gerou

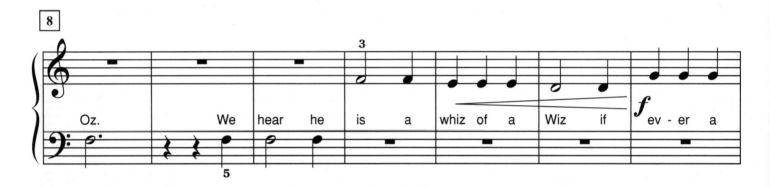

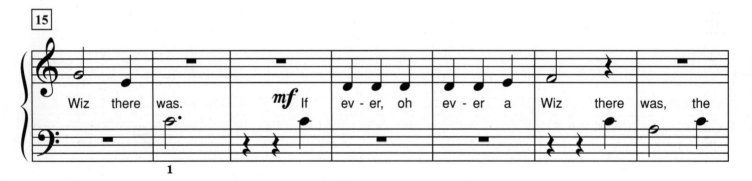

Optional Duet Accompaniment (Play solo part 1 octave higher than written.)

What a Wonderful World

Words and Music by
George David Weiss and Bob Thiele

Arr. by Tom Gerou

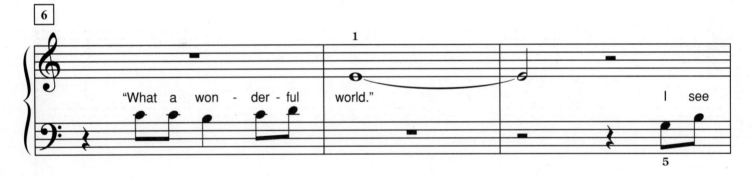

Optional Duet Accompaniment (Play solo part 1 octave higher than written.)

The Wind Beneath My Wings

from Beaches

Words and Music by
Larry Henley and Jeff Silbar

Arr. by Tom Gerou

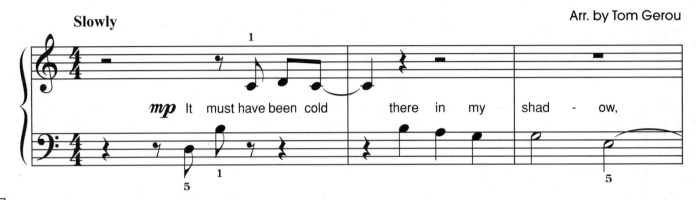

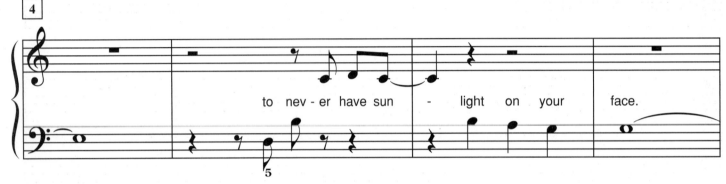

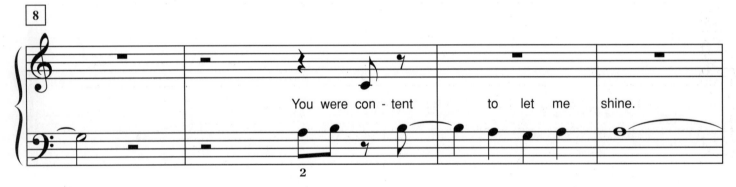

Optional Duet Accompaniment (Play solo part 1 octave higher than written.)

Wipe Out

By The Surfaris

Arr. by Tom Gerou

Optional Duet Accompaniment (Play solo part 1 octave higher than written.)

Wonder Woman

Words by Norman Gimbel
Music by Charles Fox

Arr. by Tom Gerou

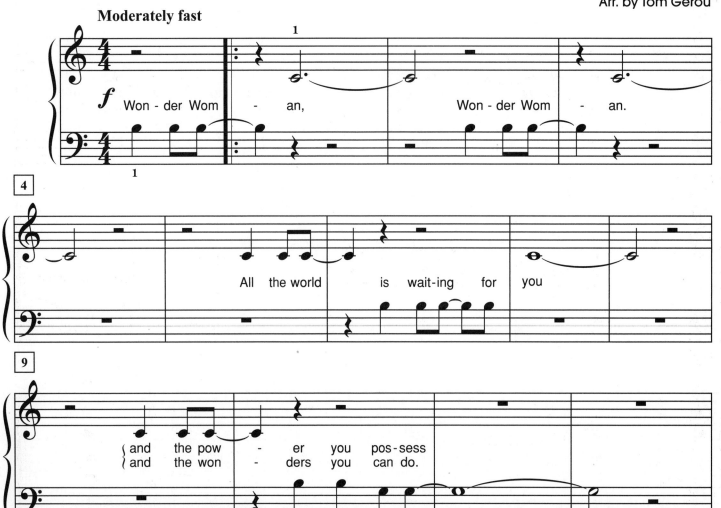

Optional Duet Accompaniment (Play solo part 1 octave higher than written.)

Yo Ho (A Pirate's Life for Me)

from Walt Disney's *Pirates of the Caribbean*

Words by Xavier Atencio
Music by George Bruns

Arr. by Tom Gerou

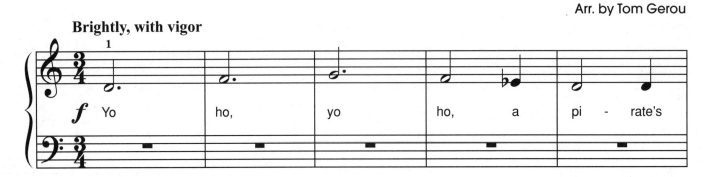

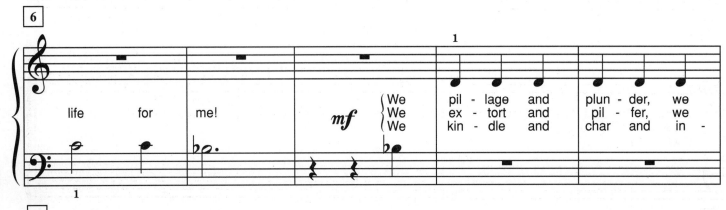

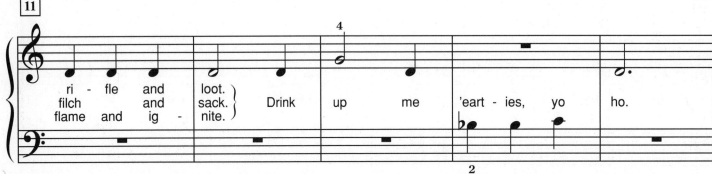

Optional Duet Accompaniment (Play solo part 1 octave higher than written.)

Zip-a-Dee-Doo-Dah

from Walt Disney's *Song of the South*

Music by Allie Wrubel
Lyrics by Ray Gilbert

Arr. by Tom Gerou

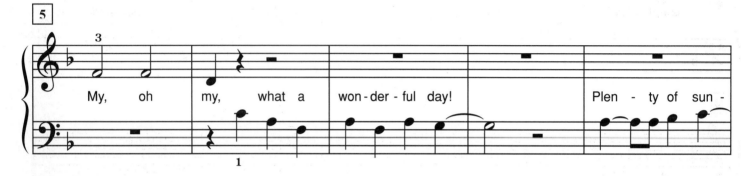

Optional Duet Accompaniment (Play solo part 1 octave higher than written.)

Happy Birthday to You

Words and Music by
Mildred J. Hill and Patty S. Hill

Arr. by Tom Gerou

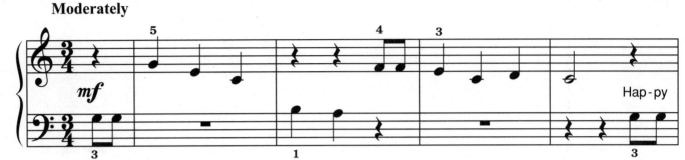

Optional Duet Accompaniment (Play solo part 1 octave higher than written.)